People in Action

FIGHTER PILOT

David Miller & Wilfred Hardy

a Salamander book

Published by Salamander Books Limited
LONDON • NEW YORK

CONTENTS

A SALAMANDER BOOK

Published by Salamander Books Ltd., 129-137 York Way, London N7 9LG, United Kingdom.

ISBN 1 85600 010 9 (hardback)
ISBN 1 85600 026 5 (paperback)

Distributed in the United Kingdom by Hodder & Stoughton Services, PO Box 6, Mill Road, Dunton Green, Sevenoaks, Kent, TN13 2XX.

CREDITS

Artwork by: Wilfred Hardy
Written by: David Miller
Edited by: Jilly Glassborow
Typeset by: Bloomsbury Graphics, London
Colour separation by: P & W Graphics, Pte. Ltd., Singapore
Printed by: Proost International Book Production, Turnhout, Belgium

INTRODUCTION

To be a fighter pilot is to have one of the most thrilling jobs available to young people today. Fighters have always been designed to fly to the very limits – faster and higher than any other aircraft. But today's fighters are so fast and manoeuvrable that they push their pilots to the very limits as well. This action-packed book tells you just what fighter pilots have to undergo, in training, on a daring mission, at sea, or escaping from a burning aircraft. Read on, and maybe one day you will be joining their ranks!

Below: A future fighter pilot trains on a turboprop (propeller-driven) Shorts Tucano, his instructor at dual controls in the seat behind him.

FIGHTER PILOT TRAINING

Fighter pilots are the 'elite' (the best) in any air force, and their training is both long and expensive.

Every air force in the world makes the young man (and, in some cases, woman) who wants to be a fighter pilot start in the same way. First, there is a strict medical examination to make sure that he is fit to cope with the stresses and strains of high speed flight. Then there are tests to find out whether he has the right character and to confirm that he has the lightning-fast reactions required.

Flying At Last!

Only when he has passed all these tests will the young man enter flight school. He starts on a simple aircraft, such as a turboprop trainer, to learn the basic art of flying. Then he graduates to a high speed jet trainer and finally to an actual fighter. He also has to learn to navigate, to use all the weapons his fighter will carry, and to fight against a 'simulated' (mock) enemy. In all, it can take at least two years from starting before the young man reaches a fighter squadron.

Right: This French student fighter pilot has moved on from basic training to flying an Alpha Jet – a high speed jet trainer.

READY FOR ACTION

Before a fighter pilot takes off on a mission a lot of preparation takes place, involving many people. First, the commanders at headquarters decide what mission is required. They then 'task' (instruct) the squadron. In turn, the squadron commander tasks the actual aircraft and pilot, and the operations officer prepares a briefing (plan).

Meanwhile the ground crew prepares the aircraft, checking that it is fully serviceable and that it has the right weapons and fuel for the mission. Having been briefed, the pilot then prepares for the flight by making a detailed plan. Finally he is ready to get dressed.

Dressed for Survival

For a fighter pilot, it is not just a case of wearing the right uniform; it is a matter of life and death! Every item of a pilot's personal kit is carefully designed to play a vital role. One essential piece of equipment is the 'G-suit' (G stands for gravity). When fighter pilots make violent turns, the force of gravity puts great pressure on their bodies, and the G-suit helps to relieve the strain this causes.

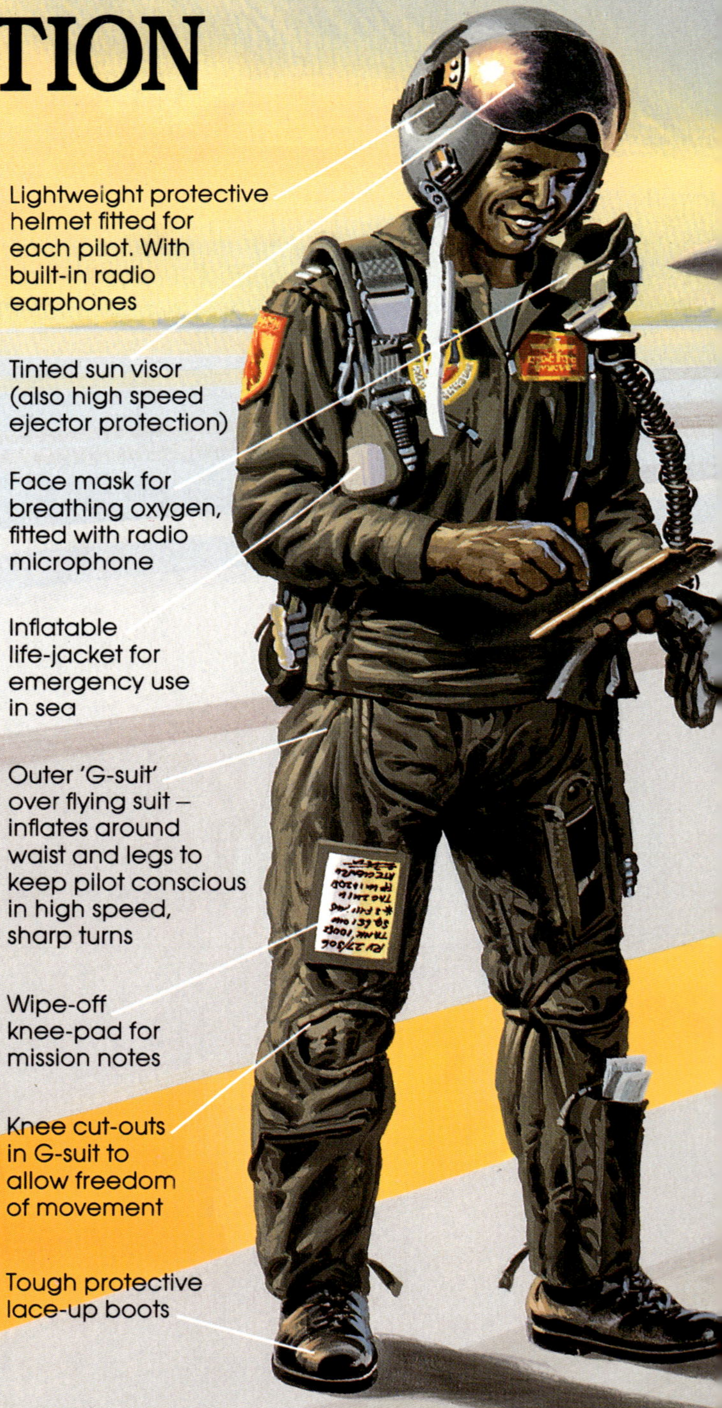

Right: Two pilots of the United States Air Force make their way towards their McDonnell-Douglas F-15 Eagle, kitted up for action.

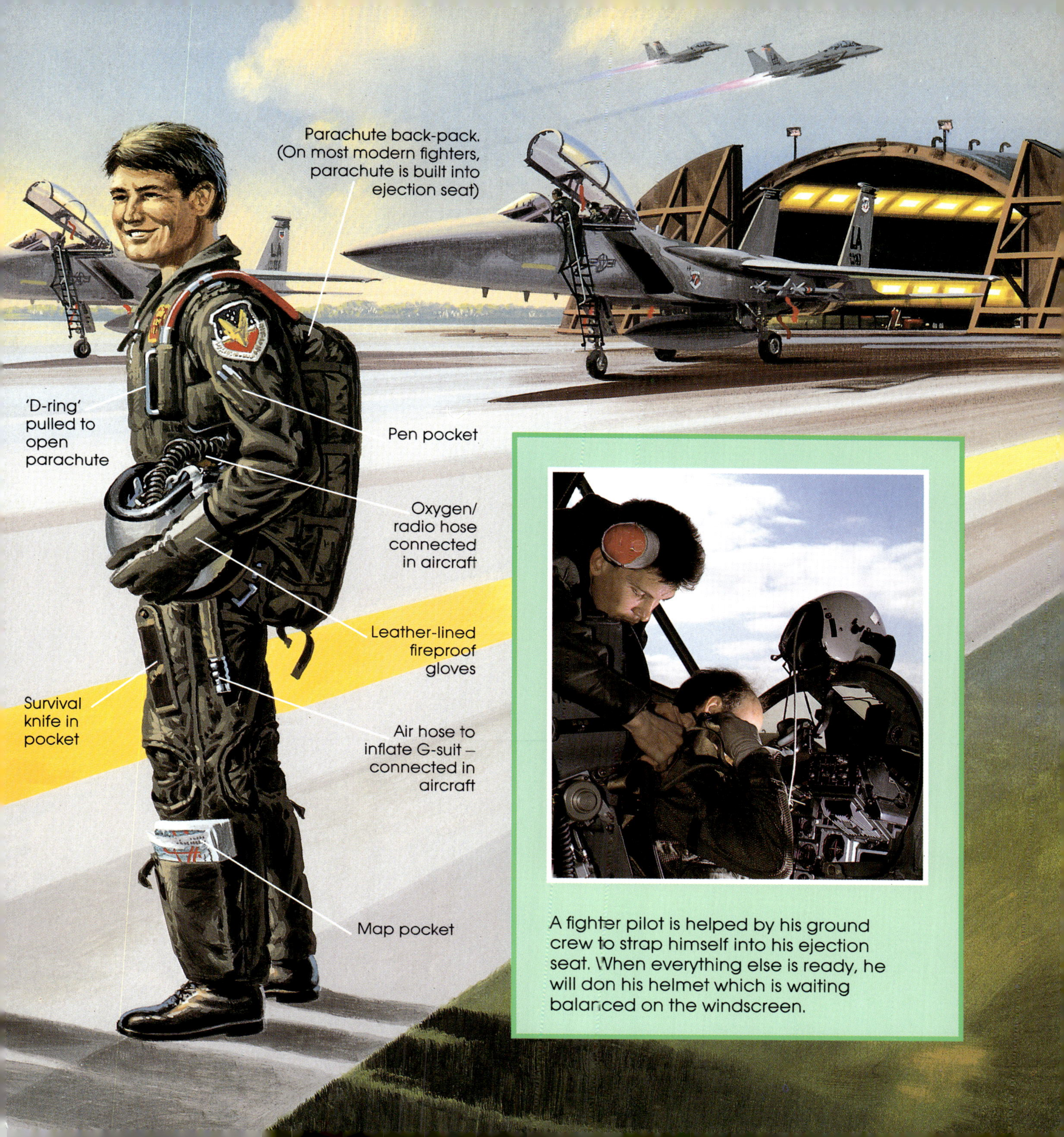

A fighter pilot is helped by his ground crew to strap himself into his ejection seat. When everything else is ready, he will don his helmet which is waiting balanced on the windscreen.

INSIDE THE COCKPIT

In the past, fighter cockpits were a mass of buttons and dials. Today's fighters, however, fly so fast and combat is so intense, that the pilot simply wouldn't have time to look down at such instruments to see what was going on. So modern technology has been used to simplify the displays and leave the pilot as free as possible to look out of the cockpit, fly his aircraft, and fight the battle!

Head-Up Display

The most important display of all is the Head-Up Display (known as the 'HUD'). This is a sheet of glass placed at an angle directly in front of the pilot. Below it is a device which projects information onto the glass – this information can be either figures or graphics such as circles or lines. These tell the pilot the speed, direction and height of the aircraft, the time to the first target, the direction in which to fly to the next target, and so on.

Because the HUD is directly in front of him and is made of glass, the pilot can either look at the display or, by slightly refocusing, look through it and out of the cockpit. At no time does he need to look down. This is vital because at modern speeds to look down even for a few seconds could easily result in a crash.

Fingertip Control

The pilot flies with one hand on the control stick and the other on the 'throttle', which controls the engine speed. In modern cockpits there is a new system called 'Hands on Throttle and Stick' (or HOTAS), in which many of the controls needed for combat are grouped onto these two devices. This enables the pilot to fight without having to take his hands off the flight controls.

Right: The pilot of a Royal Air Force Harrier 'jump-jet' has little room to move around in his cockpit.

Left: The cockpit of an F-16C Fighting Falcon. The pilot sits in a semi-reclined position which is why his feet appear to be so high.

Below: In a daring low-level flight, a fighter pilot locates some enemy tanks. Recce pilots fly low to avoid being picked up on enemy radar. They also travel at night, hidden by the cover of darkness.

SEEKING OUT THE ENEMY

One of the most important missions for a fighter pilot is 'reconnaissance', usually known as 'recce'. This involves flying over enemy territory to find out exactly where the enemy forces are, what they are doing and how many there are.

Fast and Low

Reconnaissance missions are very dangerous because if he is to escape being shot down, the pilot must fly very fast at low level.

The pilot uses various devices to help him find the enemy, including 'recce' pods carried under the wings or fuselage. These contain cameras for taking photographs, plus infra-red (heat sensitive) devices that can locate an enemy gun or tank even at night.

The aircraft may also carry devices that listen to enemy radio signals and help to locate the radio stations. Finally, the pilot himself watches out for the enemy using what is jokingly called the 'Mark One Eyeball'!

A reconnaissance pilot's view of the ground, as seen through an infra-red night vision device, as the pilot flies fast and low in the darkness to find enemy tanks.

ATTACK THE ENEMY!

For fighter pilots, one of the oldest missions is 'intercepting' – finding enemy aircraft and shooting them down. Sometimes the pilot is already in the air when a target is spotted, but, more often than not, he is waiting on the ground. He must then 'scramble' (take off as fast as possible) and climb rapidly into a position from which to attack the enemy, without himself being attacked first.

Fighters used to fire machine-guns at enemy aircraft but, today, they always fire missiles first. These are known as air-to-air missiles, or AAMs for short.

Modern AAMs are very fast, very accurate and have a devastating effect on their targets. They can be fired at targets up to 65km (40 miles) away.

Right: A Soviet pilot fires an AA-10 missile from his Sukhoi Su-27 Flanker. This aircraft is one of the best interceptors in service today, able to shoot down aircraft and cruise missiles even when they are flying very low over the ground. This is called 'look down/shoot down'.

Ready, Aim, Fire!

The fighter pilot uses the radar in his aircraft to find the enemy. Having done so, he switches on the missile's own detector which is usually either a radar or an infra-red (heat) seeker. When the missile has found the target it 'locks-on' and a signal in the cockpit tells the pilot that the missile is ready to go. The pilot then checks with a device known as 'identification friend or foe' (IFF) to make sure that the target is not on his own side. Finally, he presses the firing button.

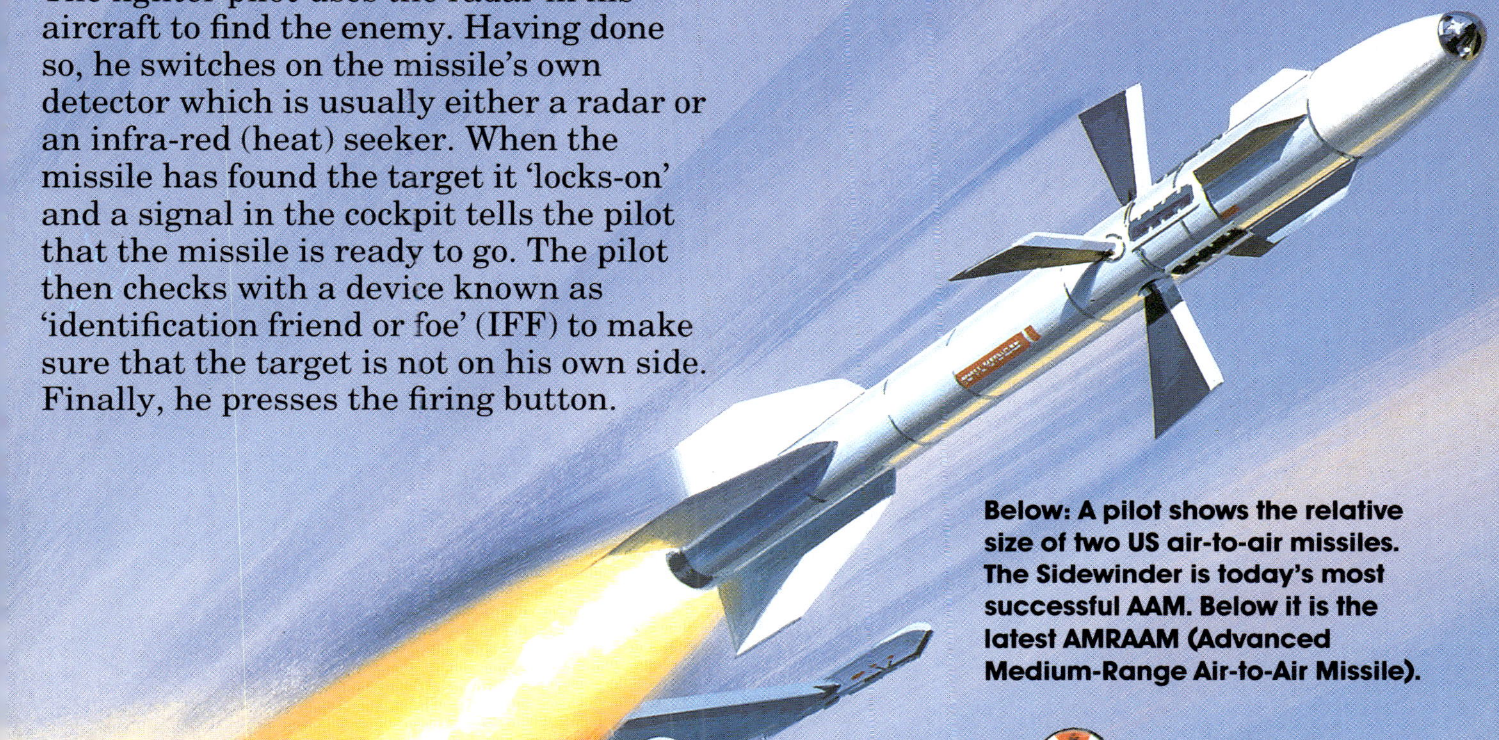

Below: A pilot shows the relative size of two US air-to-air missiles. The Sidewinder is today's most successful AAM. Below it is the latest AMRAAM (Advanced Medium-Range Air-to-Air Missile).

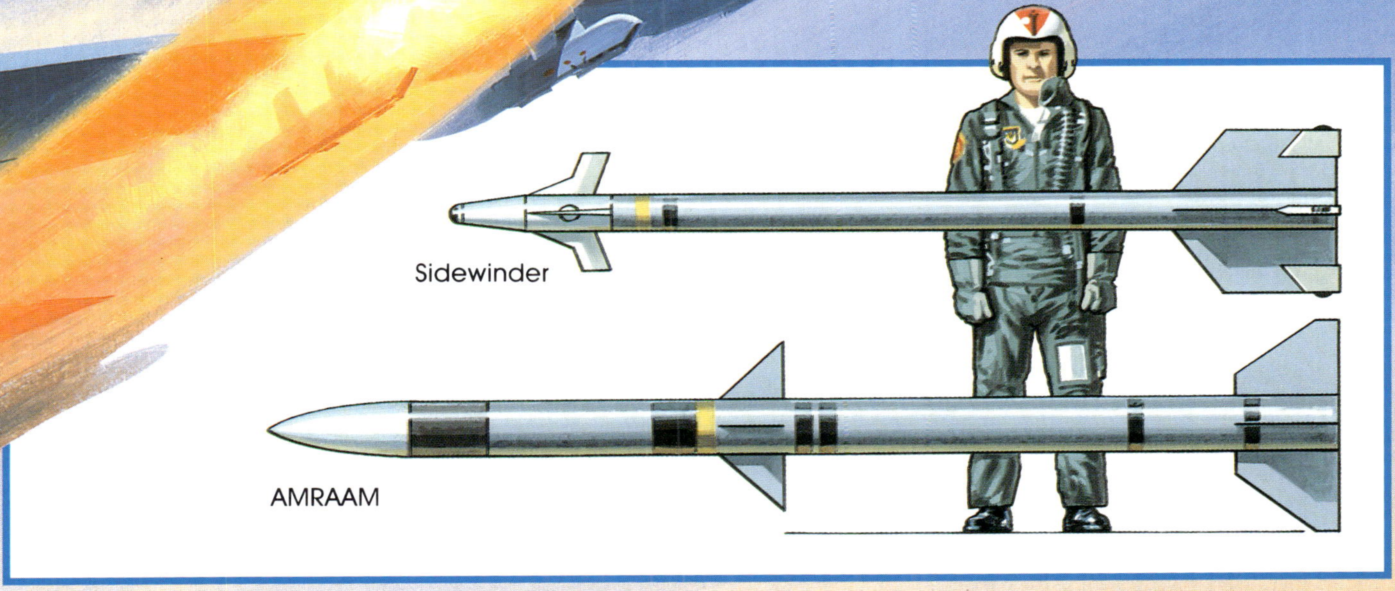

DOGFIGHTING

A fighter pilot always tries to destroy enemy aircraft with missiles, keeping as far away from the target as possible. This usually works against larger and slower targets. In combat between fast and manoeuvrable fighters however, the pilot usually ends up in a 'dogfight' – a desperate close-in battle, with one man and his aircraft pitted against another.

Sneaking Up On the Enemy
Historically, in four out of five cases of aircraft shot down by fighters, the pilot never saw his opponent before he was hit! A fighter pilot's first goal is, therefore, to surprise his enemy by getting within firing range without being seen. Equally, the fighter pilot must make sure that the enemy does not sneak up on *him*. Once a pilot gets close enough to his opponent, he uses his cannon. But rather than firing directly at the enemy, he fires ahead to create a 'wall of steel' for the enemy to fly into. In other words, the aircraft hits the bullets rather than the bullets hitting the aircraft!

Right: In a practice dogfight, a United States Navy F-14A Tomcat (nearest the camera) gets into a perfect firing position on an F-4 Phantom.

Below: Its mighty afterburner blazing, a Mirage 2000 blasts into an attack position on a Mig-29. The result of any dogfight depends on the quality of the aircraft and the skill of the pilots.

The Peak of Skill

Of course, fighter aircraft seldom, if ever, fly alone. So a dogfight usually consists of three or four aircraft on each side – perhaps even more. The sky is full of fighters climbing, diving and turning, each pilot trying to hit the enemy and to protect his friends at the same time.

It is in dogfights such as this that the fighter pilot shows the very peak of his skill and it is for this type of combat that he has spent so many years of training and practice.

'INVISIBLE' FIGHTERS

When flying a mission, a fighter pilot and his aircraft are only at risk from the enemy once they have been spotted. So a fighter that cannot be picked up on radar, and is not readily seen or heard, is most likely to complete a successful mission.

The United States Air Force decided it needed just such a fighter. The result is the odd-looking Lockheed F-117, an 'invisible' aircraft that can steal into enemy territory undetected, carry out its mission, and return to base unharmed.

Right: Two Lockheed F-117 stealth fighters carry out a ground attack using laser-guided bombs. For pilots, the F-117 is the safest fighter in the world to fly.

Scattering the Radar

When a radar signal hits an ordinary fighter much of the signal is reflected back to the radar operator (see right). But the strange, angular shape of the F-117 'stealth' fighter is designed to scatter the radar in all directions, so that the radar operator cannot detect the aircraft. Special paints are also used on the stealth fighter that absorb the radar signals.

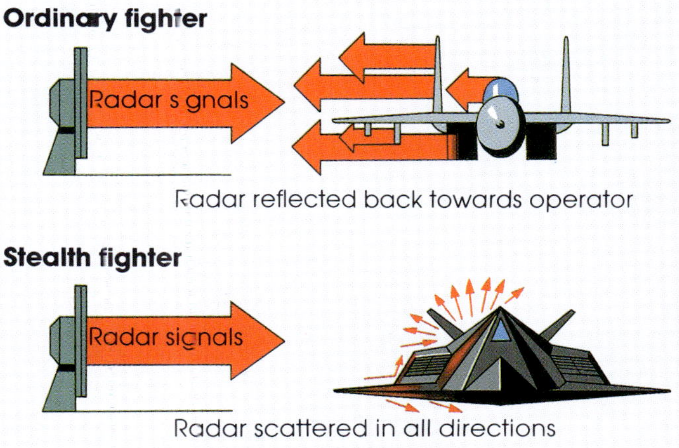

Above right: This diagram shows how radar signals are reflected back by an ordinary fighter but scattered by a stealth fighter.

FIGHTERS AT SEA

Not only do naval fighter pilots have to fly the same missions as air force pilots, they also have to operate from aircraft carriers in the middle of the ocean! Flying from carriers is a dangerous task and requires great skill – especially for take-off and landing. So naval pilots need special training to master their flying techniques.

The US Navy operates the largest fleet of carriers in the world. Each carrier operates no less than 86 aircraft – 40 of them fighters – which is more than many nations have in their entire air force.

The Flight Deck

The flight deck of an aircraft carrier is divided into three areas. The front part, in the bows of the ship, is used for take-off. Here, up to four powerful catapults, powered by steam, accelerate the aircraft to flying speed over a very short distance.

The landing area is set at an angle so that aircraft can land safely while others are taking off. There are four 'arrester' wires stretched across the landing area. When a pilot comes in to land, he uses a hook on his fighter to catch one of the wires which brings his aircraft to a very sudden standstill on the deck.

The rest of the deck is parking area.

Naval Fighter Missions

One of the most important missions for a naval fighter pilot is the Combat Air Patrol, known as the 'CAP'. In this, a pair of fighters, usually F-14 Tomcats, fly at about 150km (100 miles) from the carrier. The pilots' task is to intercept any enemy aircraft, or cruise missile, which tries to get through to attack the carrier.

Above: After a catapult launch, a US Navy fighter pilot climbs away from an aircraft carrier in his fully loaded F/A-18 Hornet.

Right: On some carriers, aircraft take off from the angled deck as well as from the bows. Here, an F-14A Tomcat thunders off the end of the angled deck, accelerated by the catapult.

Right: High above the clouds and at a speed of some 450km/h (280mph), a US Navy pilot uses all his skill to insert his refuelling probe into the drogue of a Royal Air Force Tristar tanker.

GAS-STATIONS IN THE SKY

Fighters consume a lot of fuel and, until recently, the only way of refuelling was to return to base. But this wasted time and even more fuel. So now the fuel is brought to the fighter in a tanker aircraft.

In-flight refuelling requires great skill from the pilot, who must fly his aircraft very close to the tanker and at exactly the same speed.

Most airborne tankers are converted airliners which carry huge amounts of fuel in tanks under the floor. The tanker meets up with the fighter at an arranged time and place, and refuelling begins.

A Lockheed F-117 stealth fighter refuels over the desert using the 'flying boom' method adopted by the US Air Force. The tanker is a KC-10A Extender.

Booms and Hoses

There are two methods of refuelling. The United States Air Force uses a 'flying boom'. The fighter flies up close to the tanker and the boom operator, who sits in the tail of the tanker, then guides the boom to a refuelling point on the fighter. Other air forces use a flexible hose that has a specially designed 'drogue' (cone) on the end. First the hose is unwound from the tanker. Then the fighter pilot flies to the tanker and guides a probe on his aircraft into the drogue.

Right: A Royal Air Force pilot ejects from his critically damaged RAF Harrier II, his rocket-propelled seat carrying him safely clear of the damaged aircraft.

EJECT!

If anything goes wrong with his fighter there is only one means of escape for a pilot – his ejector seat. In World War Two, fighters only flew at up to 650km/h (400mph), and in an emergency the pilot could simply jump out and open his parachute. But today's fighters fly so fast and things go wrong so rapidly that pilots need help in making a quick exit.

The Ejection Sequence
During normal flight, the ejector seat gives the pilot a good seat in the aircraft, enabling him to handle the controls in reasonable comfort. But when the pilot pulls the 'eject' handle, several things happen in quick succession.

First, the straps automatically tighten, holding the pilot firmly to the seat, and the canopy blows off so that the pilot will not be injured as he blasts off. Then a rocket motor in the ejector seat fires and the pilot is shot out of the cockpit, well clear of the aircraft. Next, small parachutes open to slow the seat down and pull out the main parachute. Finally, the ejector seat falls away and the pilot's parachute opens fully for a safe descent.

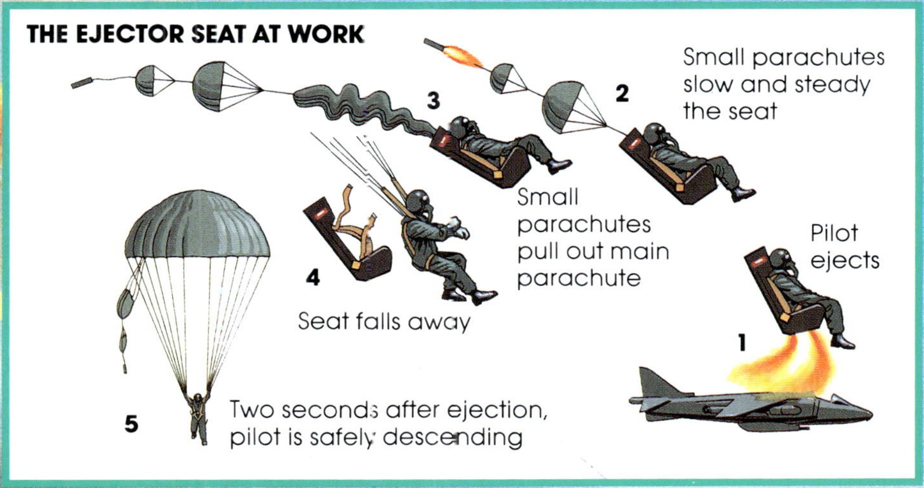

FUTURE PILOTS

Tomorrow's fighter pilots, both men and women, will be flying very exciting aircraft. There will be touch-control screens in the cockpit with realistic, full-colour displays, and talking computers that will tell the pilot what tactics to use.

Increasing Manoeuvrability

Engines will be more powerful, and will be fitted with 'thrust vectoring' (see opposite) to make the aircraft more manoeuvrable – able to turn sharper and faster than ever before. The aircraft will also be designed to be 'unstable' in flight, increasing manoeuvrability even more. Such an unstable aircraft will need a computer to help the pilot fly it.

With increased manoeuvrability, the pilot will need to wear a special, water-filled 'G-suit'. Controlled by computer, this will take the strain off his or her body during very sharp turns.

Right: Tomorrow's pilot will have visual displays in his helmet and will be able to lock missiles on to a target by simply looking at it.

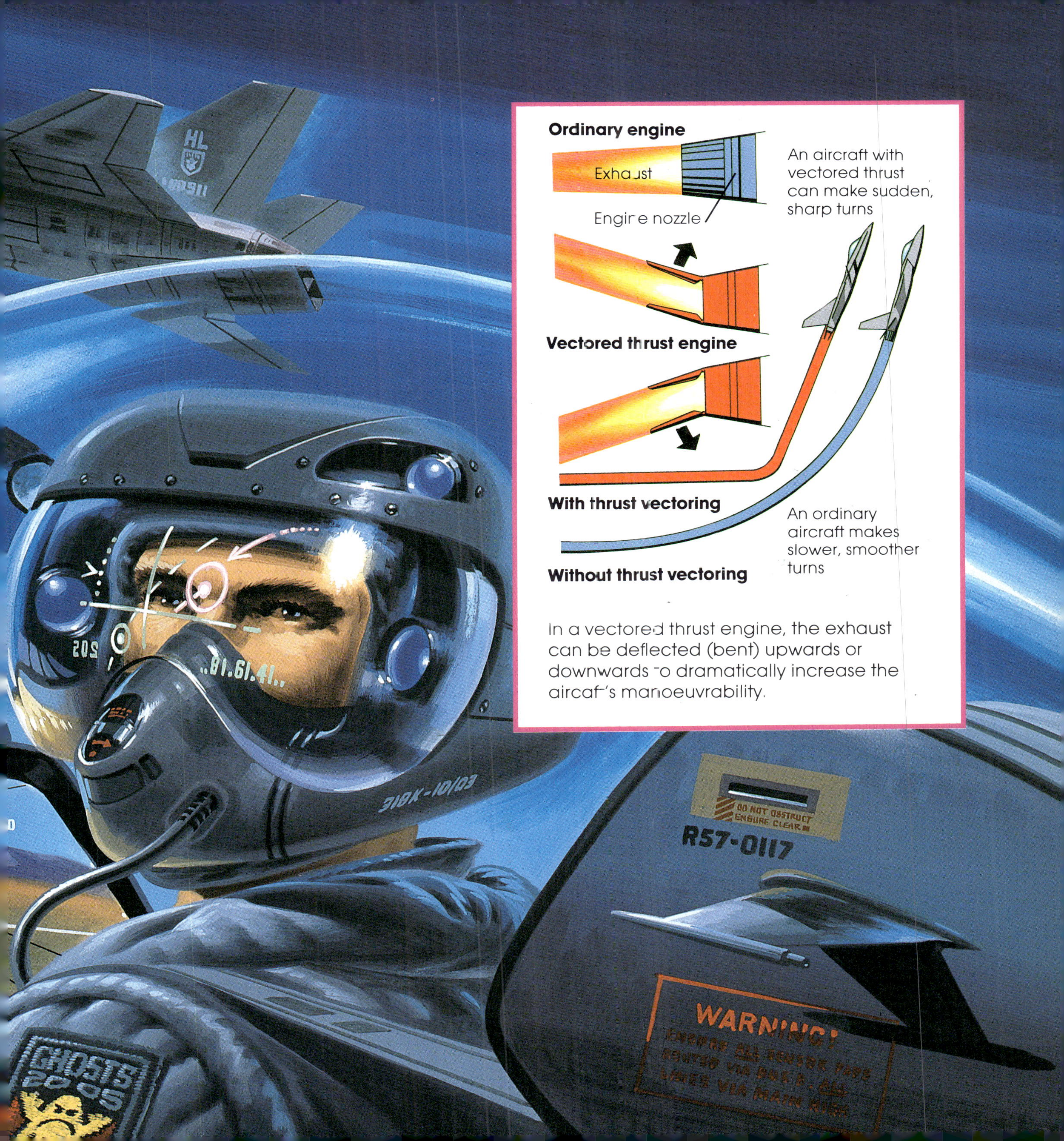

In a vectored thrust engine, the exhaust can be deflected (bent) upwards or downwards to dramatically increase the aircraft's manoeuvrability.

USEFUL TERMS

Note: Words printed in capital letters have separate entries.

AAM See MISSILE.

Afterburner An additional chamber fitted behind the combustion chambers in a TURBOJET engine in which additional fuel is burnt. It is designed to increase the thrust of the engine.

Aircraft carrier A warship with a flat upper deck from which aircraft take off and land whilst at sea. It is fitted with CATAPULTS to launch the aircraft and ARRESTER WIRES to stop them when landing.

Angled deck The landing deck of an aircraft carrier, set at an angle of 8° to the centreline. The angle enables aircraft to land while others are taking off.

Arrester wires Four strong wires stretched across the landing deck of an aircraft carrier, designed to bring aircraft to a sudden standstill. Each aircraft is fitted with a very strong hook. When landing, the pilot 'hooks' onto an arrester wire, so bringing the aircraft to a stop.

ASM See MISSILE.

Catapult A steam-powered device used on aircraft carriers to help aircraft take off over short distances. An aircraft is attached to the catapult by a strop; when the aircraft's engine is at maximum thrust the catapult is released and the aircraft is hurled forwards.

Combat air patrol One of the most important fighter missions, known as 'CAP'. A CAP usually consists of a pair of airborne fighters which remains ready to take on any mission that may arise.

Dogfight A close combat between two or more fighters. It is a desperate close-in fight with each pilot and his aircraft pitted against the other, using either short-range missiles or cannon.

Ejector seat An aircraft seat that can blast a pilot out of his aircraft at high speed in cases of emergency. When it is activated the aircraft canopy is blown off and the seat, and pilot, are thrust out of the aircraft, propelled by a rocket engine.

G-suit A special suit worn by fighter pilots. When pilots carry out violent manoeuvres their bodies become weighed-down by the force of gravity. 'G' (or gravity) suits are designed to overcome the strain this causes.

Ground attack One of the major missions for a fighter pilot, involving low-level attacks on targets such as tanks, bunkers or guns in support of army operations.

Head-up display (or HUD) An electronic device that projects flight information onto a sheet of glass in the cockpit window. It stops a fighter pilot having to look down at his instruments when flying at low level and high speed, which could be very dangerous.

IFF A device used by fighter pilots, meaning 'Identification Friend of Foe'. When a pilot detects a possible target aircraft he activates his IFF, which sends a radio signal to the other aircraft. If the aircraft is friendly the IFF signal triggers a similar device to send a reply, telling the fighter pilot not to attack. If there is no reply, or the wrong code is used, the pilot knows to attack.

Interceptor A fighter aircraft designed to take off and climb rapidly to attack high flying enemy bombers.

Mach number The number used to relate an aircraft's speed to the speed of sound. The actual speed of sound is called Mach 1; Mach 2 is twice that speed, Mach 0.90 is nine-tenths of the speed and so on.

Missile An unmanned flying device, usually powered by a rocket motor, a ramjet or a turbojet, that explodes upon hitting its target. Fighters normally carry air-to-air missiles (AAMs) to attack other aircraft or air-to-surface missiles (ASMs) to attack ground targets.

Radar A stream of radio waves sent into the sky that help detect the whereabouts of aircraft in the area. When the waves hit an aircraft some of the waves are bounced back; this returning signal (which is rather like an echo) is displayed as an illuminated spot (or 'blip') on a radar screen.

Reconnaissance Looking for the enemy, also known as 'recce'. For a fighter pilot it involves high-speed, low-level flying using infra-red sensors, cameras and his own eyes.

Scramble A rush by pilots on the ground to get airborne after enemy aircraft have been spotted.

Simulator A machine used for training pilots on the ground. An exact replica of a cockpit, coupled with computer-controlled displays, reproduces on the ground what would happen in a real fighter in the sky.

Speed of sound The speed at which sound travels. It reduces with height: at ground level it is about 1220km/h (760mph), but at 12,000metres (40,000ft) it is about 1060km/h (660mph).

Stealth fighter A modern fighter designed to avoid detection by RADAR. It does so largely by its shape, which scatters the radar waves in many directions, so reducing the return signal to an enemy radar set. The United States Air Force F-117 is a stealth fighter.

Supersonic Faster than the speed of sound, 'sonic' meaning sound and 'super' meaning 'greater than'. There are many supersonic military aircraft, but the only supersonic airliner in service today is Concorde.

Turbofan A type of engine that combines the best features of the TURBOJET and the TURBOPROP. It has oversize blades at the front of the compressor which revolve in a circular 'duct'. Most modern fighters are powered by turbofans.

Turbojet A type of engine in which a compressor drives air into combustion chambers. Here the air is mixed with fuel and burnt. The resulting hot gases escape at high speed through a turbine and drive the aircraft forwards. The turbine in turn drives the compressor.

Turboprop A type of engine in which a TURBOJET is used to drive a propeller. It is quieter than a turbojet and uses less fuel at lower speeds. Turboprops are not suitable for very high speeds.

WHAT TO DO, WHERE TO GO?

Now that you have read this book and seen how exciting a fighter pilot's life is, perhaps you would like to be one yourself. If so, the following information will give you an idea what this involves.

Air Force Requirements
Flying a fighter is one of the most skilled and demanding jobs for a pilot. So all air forces set the very highest standards when selecting people for training. Anyone applying to become a fighter pilot is tested for physical fitness, eyesight, leadership qualities, mental alertness, motivation and even aggressiveness.

Applicants must have the necessary school or college qualifications, for example the USAF (United States Air Force) requires a college degree. There are also age limitations – for the RAF (Royal Air Force) applicants must be between the ages of 17½ (for men, 18 for women) and 24; the upper age limit for the USAF is 27½. Citizenship, and how long you have lived in a country, is also taken into account. Certain air forces also have limits on body measurements such as height, length of thigh and so on. This is necessary because some fighter cockpits are so small.

Where to Start
Because the requirements differ from country to country, you must first find out exactly what requirements your own air force has. Do this by contacting your local air force recruiting office. They will be able to tell you what sort of people they are looking for and what qualifications they require. They will also give you details of their training schemes. Then you can decide if you might be right for the job, and start to prepare yourself – for example, by making sure you take the necessary examinations at school.

A Choice of Routes
There are three basic routes to becoming a fighter pilot. Firstly, with the necessary qualifications, you can apply to join an air force straight from school or college. Secondly, you can join an air force training organization at university before moving on to the air force, such as the Air Force Reserve Officer Training Corps (AFROTC) in the United States, the University Air Squadron in Britain or the Defence College in Australia. Thirdly, you can join an air force in a non-flying role and apply for pilot training later on.

Having been accepted for pilot training, your time spent as an undergraduate will depend upon which air force you have joined. In the USAF, for example, undergraduate pilot training lasts for 49 weeks, following which fighter pilots move on to fighter school. In the RAF flying training lasts 66 weeks: 18 weeks officer training, 32 weeks basic flying training and 16 weeks of advanced flying. Fighter pilots then go on fighter training.